This book
belongs to

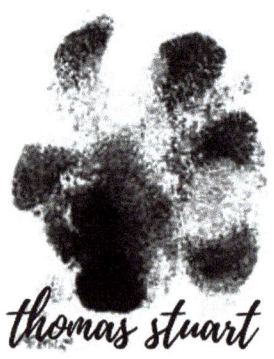

Thomas Stuart Town Cat

Cindy W. Hollingsworth

Copyright 2020 by Cindy W. Hollingsworth. All rights reserved. No part of this book may be reproduced or transmitted in any form or by any means, electronic or mechanical, including photography, recording, or any information storage and retrieval system, without permission in writing from the publisher. The only exceptions are brief excerpts and reviews.

Author: Cindy W. Hollingsworth
Illustrator: Jennifer Tipton Cappoen
Editor: Lynn Bemer Coble

Cover photo: Kim Rakes
Family photos of The Law Trio: Deanna Clark
Town's welcome-sign photo: Graham Park
All photos of Thomas and his family (unless otherwise noted): Stephanie Allen, Erica Cipko
Author's photo: Nadia Kriger-Sells

PCJunior is an imprint of **Paws and Claws Publishing, LLC.**
1589 Skeet Club Road, Suite 102 #175
High Point, NC 27265
www.PawsandClawsPublishing.com
info@pawsandclawspublishing.com

ISBN # 978-1-946198-20-4
Printed in the United States

Thank You for Thomas Stuart

I have to sincerely thank Stephanie Allen, Erica Cipko, and Attorney Chris Corbett for allowing me to tell their story of their journey with Thomas Stuart. Without their words and input, I never could have written this book. In fact this is their story, and they've graciously shared it with me for me to write. I hope beyond hope that I've shared it in a way that portrays Thomas's story as seen and lived through their eyes.

Thanks to the town of Stuart, Virginia, for having welcomed Thomas Stuart into their beautiful town nestled at the foot of the Blue Ridge Mountains.

★ ★ ★ ★ ★

Special thank you to Terri Mills for directing me to Stephanie Allen and Erica Cipko so that I could learn about Thomas's journey and life.

★ ★ ★ ★ ★

And last but not least, thank you to Cindy Joyce, the owner and director of The Patrick County Dancing Arts Center, who allows me to teach ballet to her beautiful students each week. Had I not been in Stuart to teach, I never would've met Thomas Stuart. He was outside the studio when I pulled up to work on a Thursday afternoon in September. The children were watching him, and I thought he was simply a stray cat trying to get into the studio.

It was a little while later after our dance class when I learned more about this town cat. In fact Thomas had curled up on the hood of my car. And I found him there. I was delighted.

By the time I got home and posted Thomas's picture in front of the dance studio on Facebook, I knew there was a story there that I really wanted to tell. So here it is. That very story. I hope you love it as much as I do. And I hope that Thomas, Tiny, and their three children live a long and wonderful life in the arms of the people of Stuart and the loving gentle souls of The Law Trio at Christopher A. Corbett's law office.

Thomas Stuart came
To town.
A small, grayish-black striped tabby
Just looking around.
He surely was born
Mere months before.
But he traveled alone
As he made his tour.

Where was his mother?
Where were his kin?
Where did he come from?
Where had he been?

So many questions
Town folk must have asked.
But for Thomas Stuart,
His past was his past.

He meandered down Slusher Street
Near the dance studio.
The little dancers loved on him
Rubbing his back on the go.

Thomas moved on
As dusk turned to night.
He stretched out at the courthouse.
Ah! This town seemed just right.

Stuart, Virginia,
Was the name of the town.
It was a good place,
Thomas decided, *to stay.*
Not just hang around.

"Meow, meow,"
Thomas would say,
As he greeted the town folks
Passing him on their way.

Some stopped to pet him.
Others moved on by.
But it didn't stop Thomas
From still saying hi!

But the pat on his head
Or the rub on his back
Didn't make up for the
Home that young Thomas lacked.

Living on the streets
Was hard at best.
Thomas longed for food
And a warm place to rest.

As luck would have it,
Or maybe angels touched down,
Thomas ended up at
108 North Main Street
In this hilly little town.

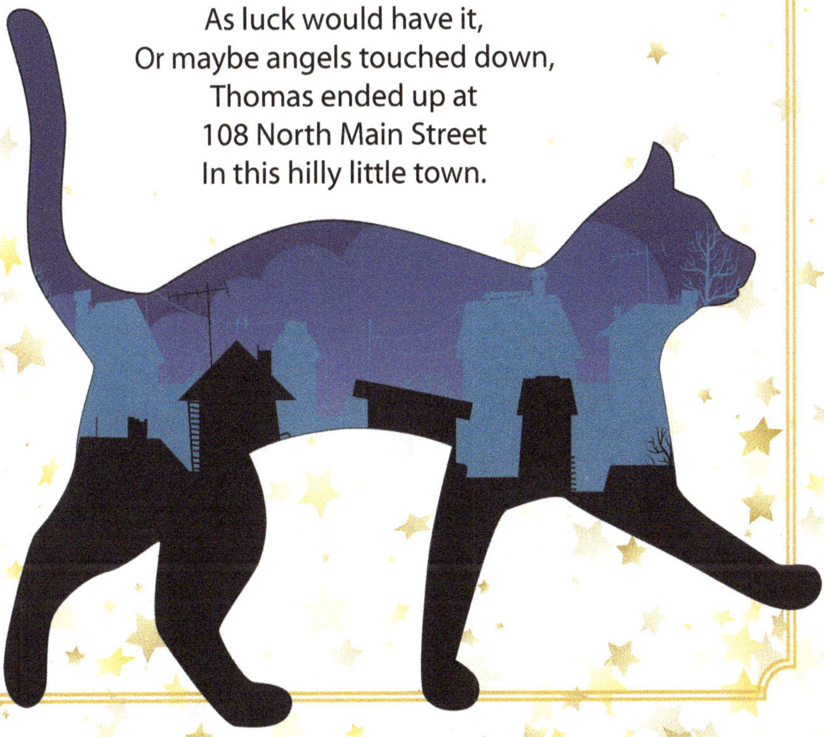

Chapter One
The Law Trio

The young striped tabby was first spotted at the back door of the law office of one Christopher A. Corbett.

It was late March. Though spring was not far off, the warmth of an inside space appealed to Thomas. The cat was tired, hungry, and in need of some care.

Stephanie Allen and Erica Cipko worked for Attorney Corbett and had noticed the stray several mornings in a row at the back-door entrance to the law office.

★ ★ ★ ★ ★

Unbeknownst to Thomas and probably to these two young women as well, a wonderful story was about to unfold. A plan was created in the hearts of these kind, loving people who saw and sought to fill the voids that were missing for this young stray cat. *Perhaps there was something missing for them as well? As with all good deeds, rewards come to those who seek to give out of true selflessness and love.*

★ ★ ★ ★ ★

Together Stephanie and Erica had made a plan. After feeding Thomas several times outside the back entrance, they waited to see how long it would take for the cat to discover that the front door was an even better way for him to access them. Yes, after getting approval from Mr. Corbett, they could allow Thomas to come into the law office for a limited time.

The cat quickly learned that when or if he pawed the clear glass door panel at the front entrance to Attorney Corbett's office, one of the two angels inside would open the door and allow him in.

Thomas found the warmth and love of the two young women appealing to say the least. He certainly knew that the food waiting inside was akin to a spoiled cat's feast.

★ ★ ★ ★ ★

Thomas didn't know any of those things when he arrived in Stuart. He was just another nameless, homeless stray cat, for which most people usually had little use or concern. But for whatever reason, the stars aligned just right for Thomas the night he came to town. Stuart, Virginia. The town he had found.

The name games.
The name games.
How much fun is that?
When trying to find
The "purr-fect" name
For this fun-loving,
Wandering cat.

Chapter Two

What's in a Name?

The stray tabby had an endearing personality and a way about him that was much more than charming. He became a regular visitor to the law office. As Stephanie, Erica, and Mr. Corbett became more attached to their frequent visitor, The Law Trio decided that he should have a name.

Since he was a tomcat, they decided Thomas was a befitting name. Because he had become more and more a noticeably, friendly pet figure in the town, he was officially given the last name of Stuart.

There in the sky that night, more stars aligned and smiled down as Thomas Stuart took on his title of *Stuart Town Cat* with a regal, yet openly friendly flair.

★ ★ ★ ★ ★

The town folks began to notice him even more. Soon the cat became a regular visitor to other businesses in the town. There the local citizens openly enjoyed having the tabby drop by. He loved getting the extra chin rubs and back scratches. His purring was an audible sign of just how much they meant to him.

Thomas varied the path he followed on any given day. Some times he visited the Mexican restaurant. At other times, the tabby strolled over to Marilyn's florist or the Honduras Coffee Shop. Many times on those visits, he even got a tasty handout.

Some days he could be found stretched out in the fading afternoon sun in front of the Commonwealth Attorney's office, the Blue Ridge Furniture store, or even the county administration building. (After all, he *was* the town cat. And—well—he'd learned a thing or two hanging out with The Law Trio at Mr. Corbett's office.)

There were days when Thomas was front and center as Mr. Corbett talked with clients on the phone advising them about whatever legal advice they needed. Yes indeedy, Thomas Stuart was learning the law ropes.

In fact, many mornings he leisurely lay atop papers of all kinds of legal doings as he stretched across the desk he and Mr. Corbett had come to share. It was a *fine* time in this former stray cat's life.

The stars knew—whether Thomas did or not—that things only were going to get finer indeed. But the cat's life was not going to be lived without some obstacles that the stars saw that Thomas had yet to overcome.

"Hey Diddle Diddle,
The cat and the fiddle."
The time had come for a change.
A short vet trip.
A surgery snip.
And calm was restored again.

Chapter Three

From Tom to Calm

Weeks went by with Thomas overseeing his new town. The tabby shone in the role of being the cat ambassador of Stuart, Virginia.

But one night another stray cat decided it was time to try and overtake Thomas Stuart's territory or perhaps even his ladylove. Tomcats are notorious for defending their digs and their love interests during mating season. On that particular night, the other cat forced Thomas into battle to maintain his position of power. No one actually witnessed the conflict.

However the next morning when Stephanie answered the meowing of Thomas at the front door, she was shocked to see one half of his face all swollen and disfigured. The Law Trio quickly decided a vet visit was needed *immediately.*

The veterinarian examined Thomas and determined that the fight had caused the injuries. Thomas needed medicine for an abscess resulting from the fight. That was when Stephanie, Erica, and Mr. Corbett decided that it was time to have Thomas neutered as well so his fighting instincts would be put out of business once and for all.

The Law Trio covered all the medical costs. Thomas stayed overnight at the vet's office after his surgery. When the trio picked him up the next day, his face was already less swollen and his tomcatting days had been taken care of too. It was the best thing for Thomas.

The tabby was good to go. He had been neutered and vaccinated against rabies and all feline diseases. He was also sporting a snazzy new flea-and-tick collar, which he seemingly didn't mind wearing at all.

He returned to the law office, and the whole gang returned to business as usual. It was almost as if Thomas were that one-in-a-million stray, feral cat that followed none of the known rules for feral cats as most humans had come to know them.

Thomas Stuart was unique, and those who met him knew it. And so did he.

Chapter Four
Thomas and Social Media

After the battle that resulted in Thomas's vet visit and his recovery from his surgery, the tabby seemed more content to stay inside the law office and just hang out. Perhaps his adventuresome wiles had been calmed by the fight injuries or more likely by his neutering. But whatever the reason, the tabby enjoyed more than ever before being with Mr. Corbett, Stephanie, and Erica during the day.

One of The Law Trio members let him into the office in the morning. Thomas hung out in various parts of the office during the day.

Cat toys lined the floors. It was as if those toys were everywhere you looked. Eventually Thomas was presented with his very own cat tree–hammock bed combination. He definitely liked that. At various times of the day and usually before the women put him out for a potty break after lunch, Thomas could be found in various sprawled-cat positions in the hammock bed of the cat tree. Sometimes one leg dangled over the side. At other times he'd be curled up in a fur ball nestled deep within the hammock. If the cat were curious about any office visitors, he might be seen with his head up and both front legs draped over the hammock's edge.

Whenever he played with his feather-dangling toy, Thomas could be seen wrapped around one of the fuzzy support poles of the cat tree. He was quite the acrobat with his many poses, as he pawed and twisted trying to get to the feather.

Thomas played and scampered up and down the hall's floors, pawing and scrapping with his favorite tiny furry gray mouse. The tabby tumbled over himself as he ran.

The "Thomas Stuart Shows," as they were dubbed, were hard to resist watching. Truth be told, those shows provided nice breaks from the daily workloads of The Law Trio.

★ ★ ★ ★ ★

Erica and Stephanie loved to take pictures of Thomas, because they were completely enamored with this tomcat that chose them to be his keepers. In fact, they established his very own social-media presence with his personal Facebook page. The women actually started the page as a means to allow the people of Stuart to post and/or read about Thomas's comings and goings and to follow all of his town-cat antics.

The women shared videos of Thomas romping up and down the hall. They staged pictures of the cat on Mr. Corbett's desk posing with law books behind him.

One day they presented Thomas with a red-and-black plaid bow tie for a more-professional business look. He obliged them by wearing it long enough for them to take the pictures. Then the cat proceeded to paw at it and roll around trying to get it off.

"Okay. Okay, Thomas," Stephanie laughed. "You don't have to wear the bow tie any longer. I'll take it off."

★ ★ ★ ★ ★

Most of the time, Thomas was tolerant with their shenanigans, like dressing him up or posing him for pictures for Facebook. However when *enough was enough,* the tabby let them know with his well-defined, cat-sulking and -fidgeting postures.

The town cat's Facebook page also helped The Law Trio keep track of where Thomas Stuart roamed when he left their office. It was a win-win situation for everyone. (Sometimes Thomas definitely could have complained that he had to suffer embarrassing and humiliating posturing just for his 'hoomans'' amusement. He was also certain he had read in some of Mr. Corbett's legal journals that he might have had a legitimate right to protest this nonsense and treatment.)

★ ★ ★ ★ ★

Nonetheless Thomas was a happy-go-lucky, fun-loving, and forgiving town pet. The cat knew in his heart that the women and Mr. Corbett loved him and were going to be there for him through thick and thin.

In fact, the *thick and thin* were just about to make their appearance.

Chapter Five
One Plus Four Equals Five

One day, as if out of the mists on the Mayo River that runs through the heart of Stuart, Thomas brought some *friends* to visit the women at the office.

It was the beginning of June. Color and life had sprung back into the foliage draped across the winding roads of this Patrick County township. Evidently Thomas had also had a hand in bringing new spring life to three young kittens who accompanied their mother to meet their father's rescuers.

"How do I love thee?"
Well, let me see.
I'll bring you
My wife and
My cute family.

Imagine the surprise on Erica's and Stephanie's faces when they opened the door for Thomas. There with him were what the women believed to be Mrs. Thomas Stuart and their three children.

Where had they come from?
Where had they been?
Yet surely, most surely,
They were Thomas's kin.

Thomas seemed unfazed by the entourage accompanying him. The mother cat and her little kittens followed Thomas's lead and joined him and The Law Trio in the law-office building.

The stars had once again aligned just right to bring open hearts and welcoming arms of love to the town's ambassador cat and his family.

Fairy tales made of stardust and pixie flights seemed almost as believable as this tale of Thomas Stuart and the sudden appearance of his wife and family.

The name games.
The name games.
Time to play them again.
"The three little kittens
[That] lost their mittens"
And their mother
As Thomas's friends.

Chapter Six

Accepting Those "Hoomans"

As the feline family adjusted to life around what Thomas called his "hoomans," so also did The Law Trio. Once again, they played the name game. Thomas's wife was named Tiny, because she was almost as small as her kittens. The three kittens were dubbed as follows based on their markings: Tiger, Spots, and Stripes.

Thomas was most at home with all of them. Some days he chose to be a doting father. On other days he chose to be more standoffish and leave the mother in charge of the kittens' care. Tiny—having been more feral than Thomas—was learning to accept the attention of the "hoomans." But most certainly she was enjoying the comfort of having adequate food, housing, and a safe space for her and their family.

Since Erica lived in an apartment over the law office, she could provide better access for the cat family to be indoors when they chose to do so as well as access to the outdoors when they needed it.

The feline family had their indoor litter boxes, beds, and toys. They had mostly free access to the halls of the apartments over the law office. All these luxuries were provided by The Law Trio.

Well, all luxuries were provided by The Law Trio *except* for the big box of 50 little, stuffed catnip mice that Jane Cardwell from the Blue Ridge Furniture store gifted to the three little kittens one day soon after their arrival. The toy mice provided romping devices for the playful "little ones," as Erica liked to call them.

Yes, Thomas was providing a great place for his family to live. And it was as if he knew that too.

Smiling stars
Were still looking down
On the good fortune
And love that poured
Through the town.
The stars brightened
The night skies.
They rejoiced in
Their success,
For the love
The law-office trio
Gave to their new pets.
Once feral cats
Roaming around.
They officially became
The Thomas Stuart Town Cat Family
Of this small town.

Chapter Seven
The Greatest Gift Is Love

Again, smiling stars nodded in agreement over their alignment and the good fortune they had sifted down upon these feral cats known as the Thomas Stuart Town Cat Family. Mr. Corbett, Stephanie, and Erica accepted the responsibility of fostering Thomas's family.

Tiny, the mother, was spayed after her kittens were weaned. Tiny was learning—just as Thomas had—that The Law Trio was there for them through the "thick and thin," as town folk might have said. After having been spayed, Tiny would no longer bear unwanted litters of kittens that would end up wandering the streets and suffering unbearable weather conditions and inadequate food supplies.

Stephanie, Erica, and Mr. Corbett knew and saw how much Thomas and Tiny loved each other. They cuddled together. They slept side by side. Thomas groomed Tiny and even appeared sometimes as though he were hugging and kissing her. They enjoyed pawing and tumbling playfully together. After all, they were mere youngsters themselves.

Tiny was becoming more and more adept at allowing human interaction. Even as this book was being written, she was still learning to be a better social cat worthy of the title of Mrs. Thomas Stuart.

Tiger was willing to allow the "hoomans" to pet her. But she still remained a bit afraid and skittish. Spots and Stripes were still mostly feral and only came around when Thomas and Tiny were present or when the whole family was being fed.

Chapter Eight

Good Citizens

With the ongoing loving support and hands-on care of Mr. Corbett's law-office trio and the Stuart town folks, Thomas and Tiny's three kittens will grow into loving feline citizens. Eventually they'll make wonderful pets for some fine folks living in the Patrick County community.

Thomas and Tiny will get to spend their adult lives loved by their rescuers and cared for by a community of the citizens of Stuart, Virginia.

Thomas Stuart will continue to perform his duties as Stuart's ambassador cat: submitting to being dressed in various garments or hats representing upcoming town festivities or holidays, checking in on various businesses on his sojourns, and appearing in photos and videos on his Facebook page. Thomas knows full well that he's special. The town folks know it too!

Thomas continues to travel his town routes interacting with whomever comes his way. He always seems to know everyone, and they seem for the most part to love his presence in their town.

Everyone who comes in contact with him feels the love he's willing to share because of the love The Law Trio was willing to give to him unconditionally. A scrappy, stray cat who just happened to land in the lap of the small town of Stuart, Virginia, one chilly March day.

Chapter Nine
...Nine Lives

Yes indeed, the tabby has been one lucky cat. *Or was it the citizens of the town of Stuart who were lucky?* Either way we all witnessed everything that has happened since he arrived. Thomas's story truly has been a remarkable series of unfolding events.

The stars did their job. Erica Cipko, Stephanie Allen, and Attorney Chris Corbett just happened to have been the designated links for the stars' alignment plan for the life of this one special, feral cat, now known as *Thomas Stuart*.

"Riddle me this.

Riddle me that."

Thomas Stuart

Is one special cat!

Postscript

🐈 🐈 🐈 Thomas Stuart lives in Stuart, Virginia, as of this writing. So does Tiny. Their remaining two kittens—Gizmo (Spots) and Oswald (Stripes)—are being socialized so that they will be ready to be "rehomed." Tiger is now named Cinnamon and has already found her "furever" home.

★ ★ ★ ★ ★

You can keep up-to-date with Thomas and his duties as Stuart Town Cat on his Facebook page.

★ ★ ★ ★ ★

Almost all of this story is true as told to me through messenger texts from Stephanie Allen. I embellished some of the story for the purpose of bringing a fairy tale–like rhyme and feel to the book. I also wanted to tell the story I was hearing from her as I was imagining it unfolding in Stuart.

★ ★ ★ ★ ★

I sincerely feel that the stars aligned for me that September day when I first laid eyes upon Thomas Stuart outside the Patrick County Dancing Arts Center. Since I am an animal lover and an animal-rights activist, I immediately felt the need to

find out why this cat was hanging out and if he had a home. My desire to find these things out led to this story. I hope that you enjoy reading it as much as I've enjoyed writing it. I simply couldn't resist the desire to bring Thomas's story to life and share it with others.

★ ★ ★ ★ ★

I'm always grateful to people who go beyond their comfort zones to help animals in need. I urge everyone to help, volunteer, donate to, or financially support those who work to change animals' lives. Support your local animal shelters, SPCA, and foster and rescue groups. Help whenever you can. Even a small donation of money or time goes a long way to help the many people who strive to make life better for animals to continue to do their important work.

Please be a responsible pet owner, and spay or neuter your pets.

May God bless them all. As the saying goes, "Saving one animal won't change the world, but it will change the world for that one animal."—Author unknown 🐈 🐈 🐈

~ Cindy Hollingsworth

About the Author

Ms. Hollingsworth began dance training at the age of three. Her first month of dancing was spent on the teacher's lap crying for her mother. But once her feet—in tiny pink ballet shoes—hit the floor, it was love at first dance. And that love has continued to this day some 70 years later. Though years have taken much from her dance agility, she still enjoys her creative and technical knowledge and uses them to continue to teach and choreograph for students in surrounding local dance studios.

Her life has been one of devotion to the dance arts and choreography and studying them all through her high school and college years. She graduated with a degree in Dance as Performing Arts from the University of North Carolina at Greensboro. During her sophomore year in college, she met and fell in love with her husband of 43 years, Ray Hollingsworth. Together they built two of the largest and best-known dance education centers in North Carolina and Virginia, and a Dance Seminar and Competition Company known as Dance Troupe, Inc. (DTI).

"My life has always been about dance and creating. Sometimes the creation leads to paths other than dance such as songwriting and writing in general, and that has been a wonderful gift. Music, theater, and the performing arts stir my soul to the highest heights of energy and enthusiasm and make living in the arts a dream come true.

"I'm delighted that through the Paws and Claws Publishing company, I have been accepted into a community of artists who write and portray their thoughts and stories through words. I'm so excited to be writing for the younger generation, the very small child. I have found a wonderful partnership with Jennifer Cappoen, my illustrator, and Lynn Bemer Coble, my editor. They've helped bring my previous books to reality. I am most thankful to God for giving me the stories and ideas that seemingly pop into my head and then flow onto the paper into the stories that will be developed and enhanced by the Paws and Claws team.

"I am also extremely excited to be able to say I'm an award-winning author. Who gets to say that? Me. I can't believe it. But thank you to my Paws and Claws team for making it possible. In December of 2016 I was selected by the Dog Writers Association of America to be in a group of five finalists for the Best Children's Book. In February 2017 I was chosen as the winner of the Maxwell Medallion and given the honor of having *Westie Tails—Meet Two Little Westies* chosen as the best Children's Book of 2016 by this association. Thank you, thank you so much. We don't get to any one place or honor in this life without the help of others. This is definitely true for this award.

"I'll have more books to come in the future. I'll continue to write as stories are given to me. I am so thankful that 'my little books' have been well received by my surrounding community and by others not only here in the United States but also across the seas.

"Life is truly about accepting and being open to new horizons, hoping to succeed but also open to the fact that failing only gives you one more advantage in the direction in which you're being led. Below is my favorite quote from Shakespeare. Thanks, William. You hit the nail on the head.

>'All the world's a stage,
>And all the men and women merely players:
>They have their exits and their entrances;
>And one man in his time plays many parts,
>His acts being seven ages….'"

www.ingramcontent.com/pod-product-compliance
Lightning Source LLC
LaVergne TN
LVHW010315070426
835510LV00024B/3399